NEPAL

DAVID PATERSON

N E P A L
THE MOUNTAINS OF HEAVEN

Introduced by Sir Edmund Hillary

MALLARD
PRESS

CONTENTS

A Marshall Edition
Edited and designed by Marshall Editions
Photographs and text © 1990 David Paterson
Introduction © 1990 Sir Edmund Hillary
First published 1990 © Marshall Editions Developments Ltd

Editor	**Carole McGlynn**
Managing Editor	**Ruth Binney**
Art Director	**John Bigg**
Design Assistant	**Jonathan Bigg**
Production	**Barry Baker**

MALLARD PRESS
An Imprint of BDD Promotional Book Company, Inc.
666 Fifth Avenue, New York, N.Y. 10103

Mallard Press and its accompanying design and logo are trademarks of BDD
Promotional Book Company, Inc.

10 9 8 7 6 5 4 3 2 1

First published in the United States of America in 1990 by The Mallard Press

ISBN: 0-792-45458-8

Typeset by Servis Filmsetting Limited, Manchester, UK
Originated by Reprocolor Llovet SA, Barcelona, Spain
Printed and bound by Cayfosa Industria Gráfica, Barcelona, Spain

To the outside world, Nepal was pictured as a Shangri-la – a hidden kingdom of great beauty where the rugged mountain people lived on for ever. The great hills were peppered with spectacular monasteries where the monks lived in complete isolation, their lives devoted to meditation and prayer.

When I first visited Nepal in 1951, the country did indeed appear to fulfil this idealized picture. There were dense forests in the lower valleys; dark green juniper shrubs clothed alpine meadows; saddhus (holy men) could be seen everywhere living in caves and under overhanging rocks on steep mountainsides, and the people were universally warm and generous.

Before long I learned that life in Nepal was not quite so simple. The numbers of children who died in their early years was devastatingly high and many of the mothers died with them. Expectancy of life was extremely low. In the remote areas there were no schools or medical facilities and life was a constant battle against a tough and unyielding environment.

As the years passed, many changes took place. Foreign trekkers and tourists entered the mountains in increasing numbers and the population expanded with great rapidity. Forests were cut for firewood and building timber and at times careless fires destroyed square miles of trees. The upper valleys became barren and desolate and severe erosion was apparent on every hillside. In the heavy rains of the monsoon season, the rivers ran red with topsoil sweeping down into the Ganges and ultimately into the Indian Ocean.

Desperate as the situation is to the experienced eye, to those who come fresh into Nepal it is still a remarkable country. The great mountains thrust defiantly into the clear blue sky – they at least have not changed. The people themselves are still remarkably friendly and hospitable. Small, tough and hardy, it is impossible not to admire their strength and sense of humour. There is a broad spread of differing cultures and religions and yet somehow the people mix together in amazing harmony.

Even a walk through the bazaars of Kathmandu is an unusual experience. You are readily accepted as part of the society, treated with cheerful warmth, made to feel at home. After a while you even ignore the rubbish and polluted drains but notice only the colourful fabrics and carpets, the great range of fruits and vegetables, the enormous variety of the people in the jostling crowds.

Kathmandu is full of diverse cultures. Beautiful temples, remarkable wooden carvings, fertile terraces clothed in a multitude of rich crops, hundreds of porters, both men and women, carrying heavy loads of firewood. And nowadays there are the trappings of civilization – ring roads, five star hotels and an international airport. I can think back to my first visit to Kathmandu in 1951 – there was only one made-up road in the middle of the city and no comfortable accommodation. There was not even a road connection down to the plains of India, so you had to walk out for a couple of days or ride a horse. But the valley of Kathmandu, a giant basin surrounded by mountain ridges, has always been a beautiful place – and it remains so to this day.

I have spent most of my time in the east of Nepal and a great deal of it in the Solu Khumbu District. The valleys of the Dudh Khosi River leads to the southern face of Mount Everest and, despite forest destruction, it is still a spectacular walk. High on the slopes of the sacred mountain Khumbila are many of the famous Sherpa villages – Namche Bazar, Khumjung, Kunde, Thami and Pangboche. On every side are superb mountain peaks known the world over. At the head of the valley is the great black triangle of the greatest of them all – Mount Everest.

We climbed Everest in 1953 and over the next 13 years reached the fierce summits of Ama Dablam, Kangtega, Tamserku and other challenging mountains. But increasingly I had become involved in cooperating with my friends the Sherpas and other Nepalese people in establishing the things they so desperately wanted. Now we have set up 25 schools, two hospitals, ten medical clinics, a multitude of bridges and fresh water pipelines, and even a couple of airfields. We have tried to re-establish the denuded forests and over the last ten years planted out a million seedlings. But trees grow slowly at high altitudes and it is a constant battle to replace the many trees that have been destroyed. At least we are trying.

The future of Nepal hangs in the balance. The great Himalayan summits could be surrounded by desert unless massive efforts are made to control the population and to protect and enlarge the forest areas. Some progress has been made but it is not enough. Only if the Government, the aid projects, the people themselves – and indeed the foreign visitors – accept the responsibility of preserving this beautiful country, will it have any hope of surviving in all its magnificent grandeur.

SIR EDMUND HILLARY

In the summer of 1979, a Japanese friend, the climber and anthropologist Kiyotomo Mikame, visited our family in Scotland. He was living in Nepal at the time, studying the Tharu tribe of the southern Terai region, and in the course of many conversations by camp fires on a trip around the Scottish Highlands, we hatched a plan that I should visit him in the autumn. The Nepalese Government had just relaxed their climbing regulations, making it much easier for small groups to stage expeditions to a specified list of peaks up to about 21,000 feet. It had been a long-standing ambition of mine to climb in the Himalayas, so we would take advantage of the new regulations and try to climb a peak in the Khumbu region, just south of Everest.

In the event, Mikame could not accompany me to Khumbu, and I made the trip alone. But in Kathmandu, his help and hospitality were invaluable as I made my preparations for the expedition, using his apartment as a base to work from, and his connections to get things done.

After my Khumbu trip, I felt compelled to stay on and visit the Annapurna region in the west of the country. This was an early symptom of a malady it took me some time to recognize – addiction to Nepal. I have since returned several times: in 1981 to Rolwaling, in 1984 to Manang, in 1987 to Ganesh, and in 1988 to Makalu. Even so, Nepal still exerts a powerful pull on me, and hardly a day goes by when I don't think of the Nepalese hills and their friendly people, and plan my future trips.

David Paterson

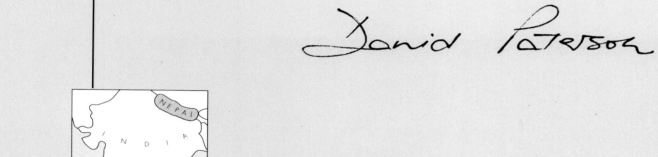

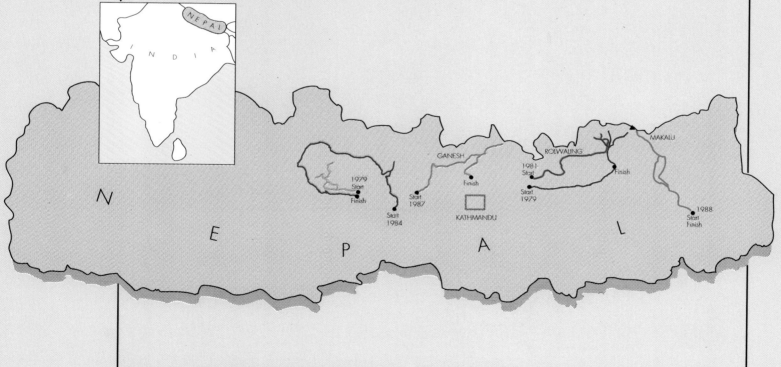

ROOF OF THE WORLD

The Everest group from Lobuche Peak

"Chomolungma" – Goddess-Mother of the Earth – is what the people of Nepal and Tibet call Mount Everest, the highest and most sought-after peak in the world. Climbers have been testing themselves against this mountain since Tibet sanctioned the first British reconnaissance in 1921. Nepal did not allow access to her territory until 1950, but the mountaineers then admitted made straight for the foot of Mount Everest, to attempt the ascent from its southern slopes.

In 1953 the joint British and New Zealand expedition placed Edmund Hillary and Sherpa Tensing on the summit of Everest and in the years since then attempts, many of them successful, have been made by climbers from all over the world. After the first expeditions came tourists and trekkers, and Nepal began to change, in order to accommodate them and their western values. Roads snaked out from Kathmandu into the foothills; hydroelectricity made its first appearance and airstrips were built in some of the remotest parts of the kingdom.

I first walked the Everest trail, en route to climb a peak called Lobuche, in the autumn of 1979. My companion and guide was Nima Wangchu Sherpa, and behind us on the trail a string of ragged porters carried climbing and photographic equipment as well as tents, cooking gear and food for several weeks. By the late 1970s trekking in the Khumbu region of Everest was already popular, but most people flew in to the airstrip at Lukla, just two days' walk from the Sherpa "capital" of Namche Bazar. Today an even greater majority fly to one of the three strips in the region; almost nobody walks all the way.

They are missing a lot. The nine or so days' walking, to where the trail meets the Dudh Khosi (the Milk River) and turns abruptly north, are some of the hardest and best in Nepal, and only a mile from the roadhead you are firmly back in Nepal's timeless countryside. The trail switchbacks, it seems endlessly, over a series of ever-higher ridges falling from the north. In between, the valleys hold a subtropical heat, and in the first days of October rice gleams green in all the fields.

Bridge over the
Dudh Khosi

I was not blessed with good weather; a late monsoon still hung around the hills and for a week we woke most days to mist and a dense, wetting rain which rarely cleared before evening. But still the beauty and scale of the country came clearly through, and on a rare fine morning there was a vista of snow peaks far to the north.

Gradually the weather began to improve, and as we turned north up the Dudh Khosi – Everest's river – this change became permanent. The landscapes were stunning and in every village there were smiling faces. In the fields, the people sang as they worked; although poor, they seemed happy and there were no obvious signs of hunger. I was falling under the spell which Nepal so easily casts and was beginning to feel, as many have done, that I had discovered paradise on earth. Each dawn the air was clearest crystal; by midday tufts of cumulous were forming, which in mid-afternoon coalesced to fill the sky; at dusk they magically dispersed. As we progressed up the valley and into the

A villager weaving a new roof of bamboo wattle

Sherpa heartlands around Namche Bazar, these clouds formed above us. Later, however, as we gained height we walked each day in afternoon mist. When we camped at 17,000 feet below Lobuche Peak the clouds filled the valley below us. Although on some days I had to toil and sweat up the trail, most of the time I seemed to float along, high on the beauty of my surroundings. Now and again, however, I would be brought sharply back to reality – with pleas for help, a sick child would be thrust before us, a boy with an open wound, a man whose swollen and discoloured leg clearly hid broken bones. Sometimes it was possible to offer first aid, but mostly all we could give was advice to go to the nearest medical post and a little money to help get them there. A couple of hours down the trail, the beauty of the landscape would have me in its spell again, but realization was dawning that for the people of Nepal it is not paradise, and that they lead hard and sometimes dangerous lives, far from medical help and often without a basic understanding of the connection between dirt and disease.

At Namche I paid off our porters with generous tips and gifts of food for their homeward journey. We shook hands warmly and they set off down the valley. Taking on Sherpa porters for the rest of the trek, we climbed from Namche into the Upper Khumbu Valley for a slow march of several days, to the foot of Lobuche Peak, about five miles southwest of Everest.

In Khumjung, just above Namche, I met a Belgian climber,

Christian Golaire, whose own plans had fallen through. Since I was alone, it made good climbing sense for us to team up, and he came with me to Lobuche. Two thousand feet above the valley floor our base camp nestled among boulders, between a glacial lake of startling greenness and high black cliffs, where red-billed alpine choughs tumbled and soared in showy aerobatics. At daybreak thin ice rimmed the lake; the peaks across the valley flushed pink and slowly changed through gold to searing white. It was the most perfectly beautiful place I had seen and for the duration of our stay we were entirely alone.

Making my faltering attempt to climb the peak, I found that I was less of a mountaineer than I had thought; to reach the top was not important – just being there was enough. Across the valley, facing our upper camp at 19,000 feet, Ama Dablam was the perfect summit of a dream; close by to the south, blue ice glinted on the steep north faces of Taweche and Cholatse; to the northwest, Everest soared above the wall of Nuptse and Lhotse. All around, a hundred other peaks, unnamed, unclimbed and unimagined, filled the horizon.

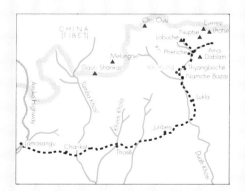

Mount Everest, with the peaks of Nuptse and Lhotse on her right, towers over the landscape. From a minor summit above the Gokyo Valley, Everest is some 15 miles distant and the view stretched from the peaks of Tibet in the north and west, as far as Makalu to the east, with foothills lost in haze far to the south.

Kingfishers dived along this stretch of the Khimti Khola river as porters made a march in the cool of early morning, shaded by steep hills on either side. Later in the day, these same hills would hold in the heat, raising humidity and temperatures to almost tropical levels.

Five days into the Everest trek, the village of Thosë lies beyond a bridge over the Khimti Khola. We camped near the school, built after Edmund Hillary's first fund-raising campaign, providing the village children with a spectacle as good as a travelling circus.

Namche Bazar lies in a
natural amphitheatre
on a ridge at over
11,000 feet, surrounded
by mountains.
Spiritual home to
Nepal's Sherpa people,
who inhabit the
northern valleys,
Namche has become
the traditional
launching point for
expeditions in the
Everest region.

Despite a decade of
tourism, many Sherpa
children were still shy
when this photograph
was taken in 1979.
They are bolder now, in
keeping with the
developments that
have taken place within
their village and the
region – the building of
roads, the advent of
hydroelectric power,
improved agricultural
methods and the
beginnings of medical
facilities.

Buddhist prayer flags snap in a stiff breeze rising from the valley of the Dudh Khosi river. In Tibetan Buddhism, one belief is that the prayers printed on the flags are sent by the wind throughout the cosmos.

On the south side of the Chukung Valley, a wall of ice stretches for several miles, to merge in the east with the peaks south of Makalu. Six great glaciers converge here, hidden by the rubble of centuries. Only the occasional crash of tumbling boulders betrays the fact that beneath lies a mass of shifting ice.

Sunset on the Nuptse—
Lhotse ridge viewed
from the Chukung
Valley below the
mountains' south faces.
At over 15,000 feet its
uninhabited floor is a
region of rocks, bare

earth and gleaming ice.
As the sun set behind
the peaks, it was
already freezing hard
down in the valley,
from where the sun was
long gone.

Above the site of our
high camp at just over
19,000 feet, the
southeast ridge rose
steeply for a few
hundred feet. Behind
the climbers, the peaks
of Taweche and
Cholatse – both around
21,000 feet and in 1979
still unclimbed – show
forbidding north faces,
seamed with blue ice
and deep in morning
shadow.

A languid drum dance interrupted the devil-dances in mid-afternoon. The cymbals and horns of the Tibetan orchestra fell silent; only the drummers played on, a quiet, insistent rhythm to which the dancers – long swathes of colour falling from hats and sleeves – swayed and pirouetted in trancelike motion.

Early in the morning, a monk checks around the inner courtyard where the dancing will be held. Later, the eight-foot Himalayan horns will make both building and listeners tremble with their penetrating and unearthly sounds.

Sherpa women and girls from nearby villages are entranced by a masked dancer at the festival of Mane Rimdu at Thyangboche Monastery. The vibrant dance-drama being performed is the central part of this most important event in the Buddhist calendar, to which the High Lama has for many years welcomed all comers.

A masked monk awaits his cue to enter the dance during the Mane Rimdu festival at Thyangboche. The monks dance for an entire day in a variety of fantastic costumes, to appease or drive out evil spirits who threaten the monastery and the region with storms, disease, crop failure and earthquakes.

The peak of Taweche looms over the yak pasture of Pheriche, and any avalanche seems destined to crash on the village. At dawn, the valley is still in darkness and streams are silenced by frost as first light breaks on the mountain's summit.

High on the southeast ridge of Lobuche Peak, we looked across its deeply-crevassed south face to the beautiful alpine peaks of Gokyo, ten miles to the west. Up here, a thin overnight dusting of powder snow had quickly evaporated in the hot sun, exposing again the ancient snows of the mountain's permanent covering.

Tucked in a hollow below Lobuche Peak, our base camp lay on the shores of a pond fed by meltwater from the snows. Across the valley, the beautiful peak of Ama Dablam was being climbed by a bigger expedition, and I would often scan its upper slopes, looking for signs of climbers.

We placed our high camp where a spur on the ridge created a flat space the size of a squash court. In the otherwise virgin snow, our footsteps of the previous day's reconnaissance lead to where the ridge abruptly steepens. Beyond the ice-ridge to the right, the peaks of the Upper Everest Basin rose in a circle of glowing summits.

Nima and Christian rest at 19,400 feet on the southeast ridge of Lobuche Peak. Sherpas are well adapted to high altitude, but even Nima found the going hard. The next day I was badly hit by high-altitude sickness (a potentially fatal condition) and we had to retreat from our high point, about 300 feet above this spot.

As the sky darkened just after sundown, a great flock of birds flew over Kongde Ri from the west, their harsh cries echoing from the hills above us. The next morning we flew out from Lukla's tiny airstrip and the Khumbu trip was over.

THE SANCTUARY

Annapurna South and Hiunchuli

A first visit to the Himalayas is a big experience for most people – few leave unchanged. I was no exception, and once back in Kathmandu after my Khumbu trip knew that I could not just go home. It was an easy decision to stay on and make a second trek with Nima, this time to the Annapurna Sanctuary, a high valley ringed by peaks over 23,000 feet.

The roadhead is Pokhara, a hot, dusty town in western Nepal. Gladly leaving it behind, we headed northwest past the Tibetan refugee camps and into open country. In the autumn fields the rice harvest was being winnowed, and lines of laden mules with bells in their scarlet harnesses ambled up the path. In the afternoon we climbed slowly away from the Pokhara Valley to a camp site high above the valley floor where cool air wafted around our tents. From the first ridge – with distant views of the Annapurnas – we plunged down into the forest, where flocks of green parakeets flashed through the trees and troupes of langur monkeys screamed at the sight of humans. Two days' walking brought us to Landrung, a neat village which faces its sister, Ghandrung, on the other side of the 3,000-foot gorge of the Modi Khola.

Across the river from Ghandrung there were fine northern views of Annapurna South, Hiunchuli and Machapuchare, but on quitting the village the walking was again through dense bamboo jungle for some days. On either side the bamboo brushed our shoulders and visibility was nil; ahead and behind us the trail disappeared within yards.

Emerging from thickets below Hinko Cave we were suddenly

in a different world. For several hundred yards the trail was wiped out by the remains of an enormous avalanche which had come down from Hiunchuli, hidden behind high cliffs to the west, killing two Japanese girls and sweeping everything – trees, rocks and scrub – into the Modi Khola. Six months later its cold waters had still not melted all the snow. Instead it had carved through the rock-hard snow a channel whose gleaming blue and white walls were studded with tree-trunks and

Machapuchare from Landrung

boulders. Impossibly foreshortened, Machapuchare rose directly from the far bank of the river, to loom 12,000 feet above. Ahead, through the last trees, were glimpses of glistening snow fields. Above Hinko the northern trail is abruptly halted by the Annapurna South Glacier, and we turned west to pitch our tents near the site of the 1957 Machapuchare expedition's base camp, only a short march below the Sanctuary proper.

Hemmed in on all sides by steep snow peaks, avalanches rumble day and night around the Sanctuary but, protected by transverse ridges below Hiunchuli and the deep trench of the South Glacier, there is little danger. Overnight snows cleansed and purified the landscape and although the sun reached us late in the valley, each day the early mists soon burned off to reveal a circle of gleaming peaks, dominated by the awesome south face of Annapurna I. Few other people appeared during our brief time in the Sanctuary and none were equipped to stay

Butterfly in the Modi Khola Valley

more than a night; for the most part, we were alone in this marvellous place.

Sadly, it is not like that today, since the accessibility of the Sanctuary (only a week's walk from Pokhara) made it extremely popular as the 1980s progressed. A row of squalid lodges, catering for trekkers, appeared near the site of the Annapurna base camp and the entire trail became heavily polluted and rubbish-strewn. Deforestation, caused by the increased need for firewood, was becoming a serious problem and in 1986 the Nepalese Government, with the help of international agencies, created ACAP – the Annapurna Conservation Area Project. Its aim was to repair some of the damage already suffered and, with the active support of the local people, to protect the entire Annapurna range and foothills for the future. With their hard work, and the cooperation of visiting trekkers, the Sanctuary and the trails leading up to it may be restored to something near their original condition.

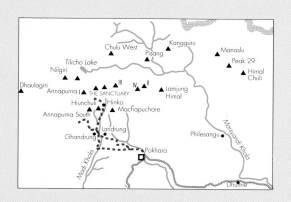

Here in the hot, low-lying valley west of Pokhara, the autumn crop of rice has been harvested, and the paddies flooded to prepare them for a winter crop. Water buffalo, highly prized for their milk, graze the boundaries between the paddies.

Ghandrung, like many villages in this region, is a model of cleanliness and neatness. Until recently the Gurung people built close-knit villages of round or oval houses with thatched roofs. Now many have switched to a more modern style, with locally-cut slate roofs and flagstoned floors and courtyards.

A Newari woman of the Pokhara Valley cradles a child on the porch of her house. Skilled as artists, craftsmen, architects and administrators, the Newars are spread throughout the central lowlands of Nepal.

Sharply defined by fresh snow, rocky ridges fall from Tent Peak and its neighbours. They loomed massively above the Sanctuary to the north, but at heights of only around 19,000 feet were dwarfed by other, more major peaks.

Giant swings are normally set up for the festival of Dasaain, in October, and both children and adults (usually men) swing fearlessly on them, to great heights.

This lady was the *namu*, or proprietor, of the tea-shop in Chomrong, where we stopped for refreshment. Wild rumours were circulating in the village that a leopard had been seen nearby the day before. Snow leopard are known still to inhabit the remoter forests of Nepal.

Turning into the Sanctuary, Annapurna South lies straight ahead. For the first few days walking up the gorge of the Modi Khola, hardly any of the mountains are visible, until you turn the corner by the Annapurna South Glacier, and in just a few paces pass through the "gates" of the Sanctuary.

First sun catches
delicate snow flutings
below the summit of
the southern spur of
Tharpu Chuli, or Tent
Peak, in the
Annapurna Sanctuary.
The spur is nicknamed
Rocky Peak, but
Sherpas and porters
like to joke by calling it
"Raki Peak" – *raki* is
alcohol.

When Annapurna I
was first climbed via its
north face, by a heroic
French expedition led
by Maurice Herzog in
1953, it was the first of
the great "eight-
thousanders" (peaks
over 8,000 metres high)
to be scaled. Twenty
years later, Chris
Bonington came to the
Sanctuary as leader of a
team which climbed
the stupendous south
face, seen here at
sunrise.

Seen from near our tents in the Sanctuary, the sun rose directly behind Machapuchare, just four miles away due east. By ten in the morning it would be high and hot enough to begin melting the night's snowfall, usually no more than a couple of inches.

An unbroken ridge of fragile beauty links the southern buttress of Annapurna III with the Gabelhorn – named for an Austrian peak – and onward to Machapuchare, just out of the picture to the right.

JOURNEY TO A HIDDEN VALLEY

Rest stop on the Drolambo Glacier

Forty miles southwest of Everest is the remote and little-visited valley of Rolwaling. Cut off by jungles to the west, a high pass to the east and mountain ranges north and south, the local Sherpa people believe it to be one of the eight "beyul" or secret valleys of the Himalayas.

I first returned to Nepal in 1981 with a friend, John Beattie, with whom I would later visit Manang and the Great Barrier. We planned to walk into Rolwaling by an unusual route, and from there cross the high Teschi Lapcha Pass to Khumbu, continuing via Namche Bazar to the alpine region of Gokyo. Nima was again to be our guide, and we hoped to see few other westerners before reaching Namche.

The first few days were routine – a steep, long climb away from the Kathmandu–Lhasa road and up into the foothills. At first the weather was punishingly hot for mid-October and I was struggling with a fever, picked up in Kathmandu. But, as compensation, along the trail the rice paddies were alive with flowers and insects and in the evening fireflies pulsed brightly in the trees around our camp. At Dolangsa, a scattering of neat houses along a hillside, we looked west across a hundred ranges of foothills toward Kathmandu. We made camp beside the village shrine and fell asleep to the rumble of a prayer wheel being turned by devout villagers.

Above Dolangsa: the Tinsang La, a mountain pass in miniature, is only 10,800 feet but a gem among passes. On either side forested slopes alternate with grassy alps and shady ponds; a final steep gradient rises to a notch in a sharp ridge and at the col the view stretches from Tibet to India, with the sensational peak, Chaduk Bhir, rising like a cathedral spire only ten miles away. At the pass, we chatted with two students walking back to school in Kathmandu, before plunging down the western slopes toward Vigu, our next objective.

Vigu Gompa is an important centre of Tibetan Buddhism, richly endowed by the people of the region and containing a treasury of rare Tibetan religious works; the monastery

Pounding millet for chang (beer)

entrance is fantastically painted in the Lhasa style. We stood in silence among chanting monks, clashing cymbals and booming Himalayan horns until their worship finished. Later we looked around the well-kept buildings and were taken to have tea in the nuns' house. An older nun sat with us, blowing on the fire and plying us with questions (which Nima translated), while in a corner of the room two giggling girls pretended not to listen. But our time in this happy place was too short.

From Vigu, the trail contoured slowly down to the Bhote Khosi (river from Tibet); we walked along bare ridges, twice crossing thousand-foot cliffs by ledges at mid-height. We strolled through lush forests – occasionally stopping to bathe under icy waterfalls – and finally followed the vast gorge of the river until the trail leapt 3,000 feet to the gates of the Rolwaling Valley. From a high ridge we looked out over the treetops of a dense jungle which stretched for some miles to where the valley walls steepened and turned sharply to the east.

That night the waters of the Rolwaling Chhu rushed by the door of the tents; across the river, a black cliff was festooned with mosses, trees and creepers in every autumn shade; behind, low hills rose to a jagged skyline. Next day we wandered slowly up to Beding, the only permanently inhabited village in Rolwaling, which is Tibetan in appearance and peopled by Sherpas. Above the village the peak of Gauri Shankar was a spear-point raised against the deepening blue sky.

After a few days spent in preparation and acclimatization – a two-day trip up to Gauri Shankar base camp, at 15,000 feet, and some exploration up the Ripimo glaciers – we were ready for the big test. At nearly 19,000 feet the Teschi Lapcha Pass is the highest in regular use in Nepal and has a bad reputation. The approach to the pass was long and hard: three miles from our last valley camp to the snout of the Trekarding Glacier, where the Tsho Rolpa – a glacial lake dammed behind the terminal moraines – held blue icebergs in its grey waters; then almost six miles up the rubble-strewn glacier in the teeth of a gale of wind and sleet. At the end of the day platforms for our tents were hacked out of the solid ice. As we crept inside, fearful

for the next day, the sun burst through dark clouds to the west; soon stars were shining from a jet-black sky and the wind had completely gone.

In the morning the real climb began. After scrambling up 500 feet of rocky rakes

The Rolwaling Chhu

and gullies we came to a vertical ice-pitch; above it, we needed to negotiate a few more hundred feet of sloping bare blue ice to reach safe ground; our porters hauled the loads while we rescued ropes and ice screws. Ahead, an alley through walls of ice led to the Drolambo Glacier: the views were breathtaking. Dizzy with altitude, we stumbled on toward the pass, still two miles away and 1,800 feet above us. Some time in the early evening we reached the top and looked down the far side into Khumbu. On the skyline those old, familiar peaks rose through a sea of cloud; we shook hands, smiles on all our faces, and headed down into the growing darkness to find a place for our tents.

There were still adventures to come – the descent from the pass; a longed-for return to Khumbu; a week in Gokyo with its perfect mountains and clear green glacial lakes; the spectacle of the Mane Rimdu festival at Thyangboche; but those were in the future. We had crossed Teschi Lapcha and were content.

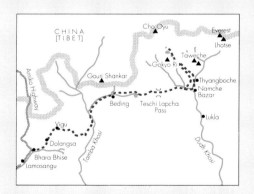

A waterfall in the lush woodlands below Dolangsa tempted us to stop for an hour or so. Although there was little sign of tree-felling, the canopy throughout the forest was open, and sunlight poured through the leaves.

We passed above the villages of Laduk and Chitre at the corner where our trail turned north into the valley of the Bhote Khosi. On these warm, southern slopes most of the harvest is already in; elsewhere the fields are still green and crops will take some time yet to ripen.

The little gompa and its chipped plaster Buddha had a neglected air. In the upper reaches of the Rolwaling Valley, Na has all the appearance of an abandoned village, but it is occupied during the summer months when the Beding people move up here with their animals.

In this spectacular entrance we waited to be taken into the main hall of Vigu Gompa. The monastery had recently been decorated by a master craftsman from Lhasa and all the religious murals, and the buildings themselves, gleamed with fresh paint.

We spent two days in Beding to begin our acclimatization before setting off to climb the Teschi Lapcha Pass. Although we got on well with its Sherpa people, there had been some recent trouble between trekkers and locals, and the area was closed soon after we passed through.

The northern slopes of the Manlung La peaks lie in Tibet, just two miles from where this shot was taken. Sadly, the beauty of our surroundings at Gauri Shankar base camp was marred by typical base-camp litter: cans, plastic containers and gas cylinders.

Our Beding porters haul loads, including firewood, up the steep ice-pitch at the snout of the Drolambo Glacier. Below them is the rubble-covered Trakarding Glacier, and beyond lie the peaks south of the Rolwaling Valley.

Above the short ice wall and a rising traverse on blue ice, a sloping ramp led to the upper Drolambo Glacier. The altitude was 17,000 feet, and there were still nearly 2,000 feet to climb to the top of the pass, some two and a half miles away.

In an area such as Rolwaling, many of the peaks do not have even local names, and most are unclimbed. These summits on the south side of the valley, rising through evening mist like the heads of prehistoric monsters, were first explored in 1952 by a Scottish expedition.

On the upper slopes of the Teschi Lapcha Pass, at over 18,000 feet, our little party began to drift apart as everyone moved at his own pace, concentrating hard to synchronize each breath and upward step. The Drolambo Glacier is now far below; the peak is Dragkar Go, its rock walls too steep to hold snow.

In the fading afternoon sun, our porters and those of a Swiss group make a last effort up the final slopes to the col, where many prayed. We had encountered the Swiss party down in the valley at Na, and agreed to join forces for the two crucial days crossing Teschi Lapcha.

We stayed at the col until the sun was gone and the air was chill. Down below beetling cliffs, the Swiss group had already occupied the best-protected sites for tents. We were condemned to a night spent listening to stones and lumps of ice whistle down from the heights above to impact in the snow only yards from where we lay.

73

Above the Gokyo lakes, a minor 18,000-foot peak gives a 360-degree panorama. Looking southeast to Cholatse and Taweche, the lake below is green due to minerals leeched from the rock of the surrounding mountains. In the distance, the daily raft of cloud is slowly forming in the lower valley.

A freezing mist rises from the lake at Gokyo, where we were camped beside the stone corrals of a yak pasture. The altitude, almost 15,500 feet, marks the limit of even temporary summer habitation and animal pasture here in east Nepal. The peak across the lake is Gokyo Ri.

Above the high yak pasture at Maccherma, Gokyo Ri is one of two beautiful peaks which rise from a system of miniature valleys and glaciers, alpine in scale. At this season Maccherma was deserted, since the Sherpa people had returned to their lower, warmer quarters for the winter.

THE GREAT BARRIER

Annapurna II seen from the east

In 1984 I returned to the Annapurna region. In five years the number of people trekking in Nepal had grown enormously; some areas had been closed, including Rolwaling which I had visited two years previously. There was even talk of the Everest region being restricted for some years to allow for regeneration. But the long trail around the Annapurnas was still open and I had come with John, my Scottish partner, to trek this route with some variations. For once Nima couldn't be with me, and we had a new guide, Dende.

The trails here were busy from the start, with many local people returning to their home villages for the festival of Dasaain and all headed the same way as ourselves. Soon we were ready to get on to a quieter trail, and opted for a route leading up below the peaks of Manaslu Himal. In two days we climbed nearly 12,000 feet, at first in scorching heat across steeply-terraced hillsides, but later through cool cloud forest of pine, cedar, oak and giant rhododendron. High on the ridge two tiny blackwater lakes lay cupped in hollows among the trees, tempting us to stop. But we did not like their stagnant look, and continued high above the treeline in the search for clean water and a place to camp. Next morning at dawn Manaslu soared above us to the north, rose-pink against a violet sky; to the west, Machapuchare and the Annapurna range reared out of brown plains and foothills in a distant haze.

From there the only way was down, back to the main trail, to follow the course of the Marsyandi River north and west as it cut through the Himalayan chain on the way from Manang and its source in the snows above Tilicho Lake. For a time we savoured the pleasures of the lower valleys – bright butterflies and the sight and sounds of exotic birds, warm side streams to bathe in, the lazy evening rituals of reading, writing, conversation and cigarettes around a camp fire.

The Manang Valley, when we reached it, was a colder, harder place and well deserved its nickname of "Little Tibet". A ceaseless wind blew down the middle of an almost treeless valley, carrying a stinging load of dust and grit and tearing smoke from the flat roofs of a shuttered village; deeply eroded slopes descended from pine-clad ridges leading, in the north, to the brown hills of the Tibetan border. For more than 25 miles along the south side of the valley the entire Annapurna range raised an unbroken wall of snow, ice and rock, never falling below 20,000 feet – the Great Barrier.

The monastery of Braga was padlocked and deserted when we tried to visit, and the village of Manang itself unkempt and dirty. After a day to rest and regroup, we headed back into the hills, this time due north toward the peaks of Chulu and the

Carved mane stone, Pisang

lands along the border with Tibet.

I had hoped to reach the Kang La, a pass to the east of the Chulu range, but a two-day march past eerily-deserted villages and through empty hills left us on the brink of a drop not marked on any map, and with the pass far on the other side. Behind us two pale blue lakes

Paddy-field frog,
Pokhara Valley

lay on a shelf of rock above the great void of the Manang Valley. Beyond was the Barrier, stretching from horizon to horizon; Lamjung Himal at the far eastern end of the range, then Annapurnas II, IV and III, Gangapurna, Glacier Dome, Roc Noir and Tilicho Peak. Much farther off to east and west, and lost in haze, were the two giants, Manaslu and Dhaulagiri.

It was a perfect place to make camp, and for several days we explored the ridges and minor peaks above our tents. The air sparkled and at 16,000 feet the night frost was keen. The downhill walk to Manang took only a day, and from there we headed over the 17,500-foot Thorong La (pass). Even at this late season the trail was clear of snow; at the pass a desert of black stone stretched to the foot of ice-clad peaks; a bitter wind blew in our faces. It was no place to loiter, and we strode off down the western slopes into Mustang, leaving the Buddhist highlands behind us, and Pokhara and the twentieth century were only a week's walk away.

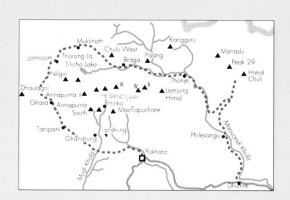

Two teenage boys walk home through the autumn rice crop near their village in the Marsyandi Valley. These hot, fertile valleys easily support two crops a year, the second being harvested in November.

In the hills of Nepal, the narrow terraced fields are tilled with oxen and probably always will be. But roads are now being driven up the main valleys and mechanized transport introduced, and in places such as the lower Marsyandi Valley, the days of traditional farming methods may soon be over.

It was the last day of Dasaain in Bahundanda, and everyone was in festive mood. Although it is enjoyable to camp while trekking, lodges like this exist along many of the busier trails and most are generally clean, very simple and pleasantly cool.

The passage of evil spirits along the trail is prevented by this shaman's doll near the village of Jagat. In the countryside of Nepal, animism and shamanism still coexist with the main religions. People also revere the natural world equally with their countless gods and goddesses.

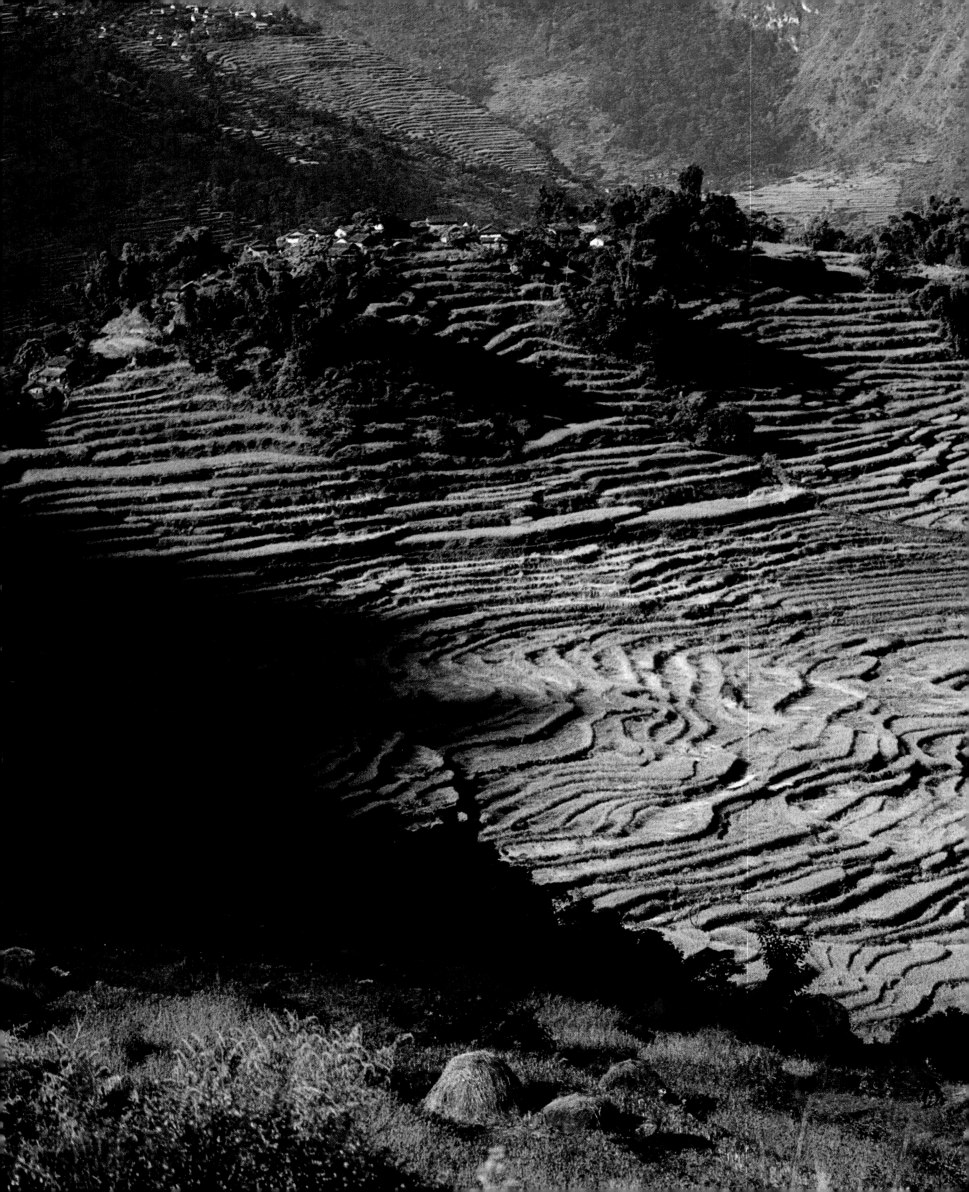

Climbing away from the Marsyandi Valley, en route to the ridges below Himalchuli, we passed through an area where the sculptured terraces were particularly fine. The trails and villages were now quiet; most people were indoors celebrating the festival with their families.

At 12,000 feet on the Bara Pokhari Lekh (Big Lake Ridge) the Manaslu group was still far distant. Manaslu on the left is one of the fourteen 8,000-metre peaks in the world; her southern neighbours, Peak 29 and Himalchuli, are also giants.

High up in the Manang Valley there is an important monastery at Braga. On the approach to this auspicious site, the mane stones and walls, the chortens, and prayer walls like this begin to appear. The wall is set along its length with inscribed metal prayer wheels, to be turned by hand by someone walking clockwise around it.

The clouds flushed pink as the moon rose above Annapurna II, and a ruby glow stayed in the sky until long after the Manang Valley had disappeared in evening gloom. It was the promise of fine weather we wanted before setting off next day to cross the Thorong Pass.

The brown, eroded slopes below Pisang Peak (19,950 feet) are more like the landscape of Tibet than Nepal. Manang lies north of the main Himalayan chain and, because the monsoon breaks against the mountains, the land to the north is in rain shadow and remains dry and bare.

From 15,000 feet on the north side of the Manang Valley, our camp looked south to the Annapurnas. Directly opposite, the upper slopes of Annapurna III caught the first light of the rising sun, around 6am. By mid-morning, these north-facing slopes would be in deepest shadow.

The silhouette of Thorong Peak at the western head of the valley indicated the route we would take on leaving Manang. At its highest point, the trail through the pass is only a little lower than this summit.

Autumn was shading into winter as we left our high camp above Manang and the lakes were frozen, probably to stay that way until the spring. Across the valley, Annapurna and Gangapurna are named for Hindu goddesses of great power.

Below the Gangapurna Glacier, a tear-shaped lake gathers the snow melt. As we climbed north into the hills above Manang, more and more of the Great Barrier came into view. Here, Gangapurna, Roc Noir and Tilicho Peak mark its western limits.

96

The Thorong La lies
between Manang and
Mustang and, despite
its height of over 17,500
feet, for most of the
year it is clear of snow.
Heading west, soon
after crossing the
summit, the village of
Muktinath comes into
view, 5,000 feet below.
Reaching it involves a
punishing three-hour
descent.

The old caravanserai at
Muktinath is an
overnight shelter for
pack animals on the
route from Pokhara to
Manang, via Jomosom.
This trail climbs to
more than 17,500 feet,
to cross the Thorong
La. But, unlike the
great majority of trails
in Nepal which are too
precipitous to allow the
use of animals, it is
never dangerously
steep.

Near Muktinath on the eastern border of the forbidden region of Mustang, the fortified village of Jharkot is sensationally situated at the end of a ridge amid bare, brown hills. Mustang has long been a source of friction between Nepal and Tibet, and armed skirmishes involving Nepali troops and Khampa rebels were still occurring in the early 1970s.

Flat-roofed and wooden-shuttered, the houses of Jharkot show strong Tibetan influence. The people of this region are mainly Thakalis who migrated south from Tibet some hundreds of years ago, at the same time as the Sherpas.

101

In mountain areas everywhere, the formation of fish- or saucer-shaped clouds – like this one over Dhaulagiri – is taken as a sign of bad weather. As we continued down into the gorge of the Kali Gandaki river, this portent turned out to be true, and on three consecutive nights snow fell heavily, right down into the valley.

WALKING OFF THE MAP

First sun on Himalchuli

We were definitely lost. Two hours of searching up and down the heavily-forested ridge had produced nothing but animal trails which petered out above high, crumbling cliffs. There was no onward trail, and to turn south down the ridge, losing painfully-gained altitude, seemed to be the only way out; a chance meeting with a raffish band of hunters confirmed this. (Our only map was proving hopelessly inaccurate, and would be of little use throughout the trek.) The hunters cheerfully declined to be photographed: they had no licences for their ancient weapons and the bear, leopard and musk deer they claimed to be hunting are all protected in Nepal. We shook hands and set off downhill.

This incident set the pattern for what became an extremely arduous trek. Nima and I had come in the spring of 1987 with a friend, Mike McQueen, another photographer, aiming to get away from conventional trekking routes. Ganesh Himal was one of the least-known areas.

We set off from Gorkha, an ancient capital of Nepal, now just another dusty bazaar town in the lower foothills, and it was soon clear that conditions here were quite different to other parts of Nepal that I had seen. Entire hillsides were treeless; the shade-trees which traditionally line the trails were gone, and in some villages even the great pipul tree, around which the houses are grouped, had been cut down, presumably for firewood. Ten days later, unable to buy supplies for our porters, we learned that there was a food shortage in the area, caused by several poor harvests, and Government supplies were being distributed to prevent famine. We got by, sharing out what we had until we left the region, but it was the first time I had seen this problem in Nepal and it was disturbing.

Five thousand feet up, five thousand feet down; high, cool forests with wreaths of old snow under the trees alternated with subtropical jungles of suffocating humidity, humming with insects, echoing with bird calls and alive with butterflies. Villages were few and the people, who call themselves the Ghalë, were shy. When we finally turned north up the Ankhu River toward the mountains, we were already a little dispirited,

knowing that the decision to turn south that day in the forest had been mistaken. Five days' strenuous march later we were hardly any nearer to Ganesh Himal and the country itself had made clear what the map had not – that first ridge had led straight to the heart of the

Mike and Khyimjung, Langtang

Ganesh range. We were now much too far south.

Another three days on, and stuck high on a hill in a 15-hour thunderstorm, we agreed to abandon our attempt to get right into Ganesh Himal. Earlier in the day, we had been beaten by a combination of thorn scrub, trackless forest, and dangerous, loose climbing. The weather, freakish since the start, had sapped our energy with its intense heat and humidity and its vicious storms. We had hardly even seen the mountains, now only five miles distant, because of thick haze. I insisted on one more night in this camp, believing our luck would change.

Rhododendrons frame
Langtang Lirung

Morning brought the hoped-for clearance – above us, Ganesh II and V rose through the last remnants of cloud; southward, down the valleys toward Trisuli, we could see vast distances for the first time. But decisions had been made, so we broke camp and left. Descending 5,000 feet to cross the Monjar River, climbing up to the Pangsung Pass at 12,500 feet, then down to the Mailung Khola, and up again to the Paldol Pass – it was a replay of the first part of the trek, but with heavy overnight snows and only the shattered timbers of an abandoned village at Mailung Pati to hint at any human presence. Ice crystals clung to scarlet rhododendrons as we searched in vain for a trail to take us to the final pass; we turned uphill through the trees in hope.

An hour later, to our complete astonishment, we stood on a wide dirt road cutting through the pines. This, we were to find, was a road into Ganesh, being built by the Nepalese army, leading to the site of commercial deposits of bauxite, rubies and, it was rumoured, uranium. Whatever its purpose, it seemed a totally alien presence in this landscape and as we headed on into Langtang, we could see its ugly scar across miles of previously virgin forest.

Crossing the great Trisuli River we met two trekkers – our first for over two weeks. The Langtang Valley is a National Park and, even before the new road was pushed through, it was a popular destination. We planned to walk to Kyanjin Gompa, at the head of the valley, and out over the 17,000-foot Kangja

La (pass), to take a direct southern route to Kathmandu. The valley, as expected, was relatively busy with trekkers, but the wild scenery compensated as we made the two-day journey up to the gompa. Walking first through woods of oak, azalea and rhododendron, the country got bleaker as we climbed; finally the Langtang River ran down a bare valley below black cliffs.

We camped at 13,000 feet on the lower slopes of Langtang Lirung and spent one glorious day walking the snow-covered ridges and minor peaks on the north side of the valley. But yet more climbing plans were to be frustrated. Waking the next morning to six inches of fresh snow, and more falling thickly from a leaden sky, we spent a day looking anxiously at the weather and shaking the snow from sagging tents. Another day dawned to more snow and heavier clouds; on the toss of a coin, we packed up quickly and set off downhill.

Three days later we hitched a ride on a truck heading south along the new road, and the next night were in Kathmandu. Ganesh had been a learning experience and the idylls of my previous travels in Nepal had been placed in a new perspective.

The steepness of these terraced fields near Hindung in the Ganesh foothills is betrayed by the lack of houses. Nepal's rapidly increasing population, coupled with steady immigration from India, means that more and more land – even such dizzy slopes as these – must be brought under cultivation.

In all the fields between
Gorkha and Arughat
Bazar, rice had been
newly planted and the
paddies flooded. This
was a welcome sight in
an otherwise parched
landscape, and local
people were hoping
that heavy spring rains
would offset the effects
of two failed monsoons.

These three Gurung-
Ghalë girls were
carrying enormous
loads of ceramic pots
back to their home
village in the upper

Buri Gandaki Valley.
Shy at first to be
photographed, they
relaxed as we chatted
over cups of tea and
cigarettes.

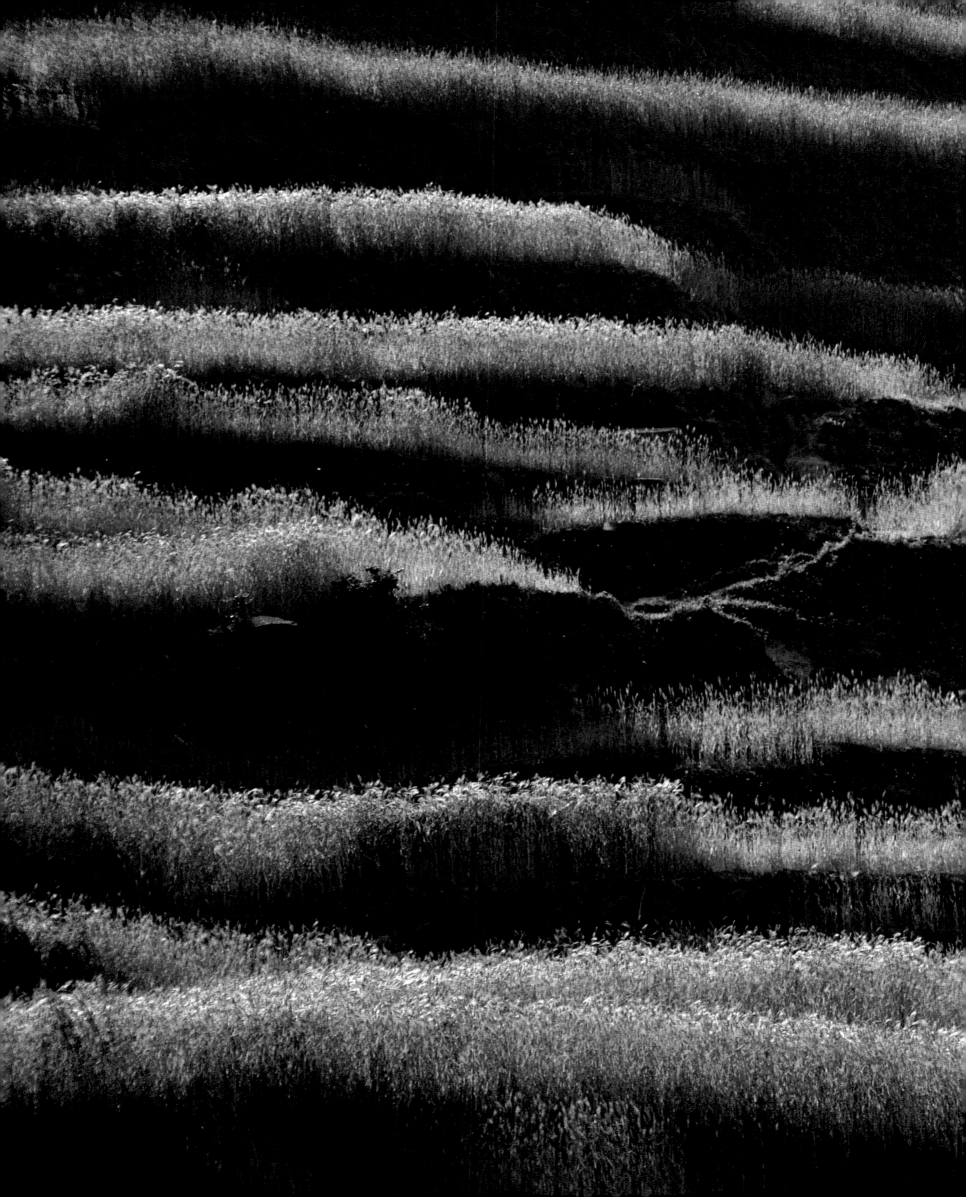

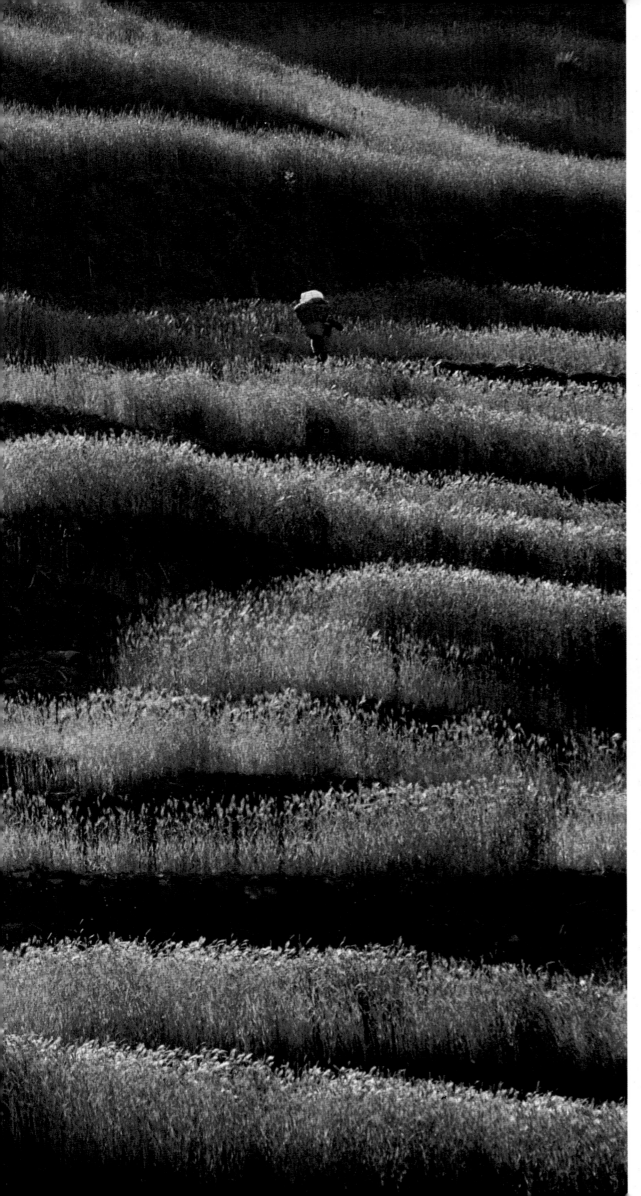

Between slowly ripening fields of winter wheat above Runchet, our porters walk on paths no wider than a man's foot. Higher up, the crops are of barley and hardy millet; at the upper limits of cultivation, only potatoes can be grown.

Winter crops near Gorkha have already been harvested and the empty fields show even more clearly how the sculptured terraces follow the natural contours of the land. A research station not far from here investigates new strains of crops, and works on the fastest way to reafforest areas suffering severe tree loss.

113

Khading, in the
southern Ganesh
foothills, is one of the
few villages in an area
of extreme poverty.
But the people are as
cheerful and vivacious
as elsewhere in Nepal:
they entertained us
with a concert the
evening we arrived,
hoping for a
contribution to their
school fund.

Vigorous young
rhododendron bushes
grow below fire-
damaged trees near the
top of the 12,000-foot
Pangsung Pass below
Ganesh IV. These fires
most probably resulted
from lightning strikes
– a common hazard in
forested areas – rather
than from slash-and-
burn cultivation as
elsewhere.

Densely wooded ridges above our camp in the Mailung Khola Valley were softened by early morning haze. The trail we had followed here was very indistinct, and at Mailung Pati we had hoped to find some houses and get directions. But only rubble and abandoned roof timbers protruded through the snow.

A Tamang villager, wearing a cloak of woven straw against the early-morning cold, comes to inspect our camp on the Abuthum Ridge just after dawn. We had arrived in darkness the previous night, and woke to the breathtaking views of Manaslu Himal, 25 miles to the northwest.

The south face of
Ganesh II gleams with
fresh snow after two
days of storms which,
lower down the valley,
we experienced as
thunder, lightning and
torrential rain. Below
the peak was the
narrow gorge of the
Ankhu Khola, which
had offered no route
into the mountains.

The Gurung hill-tribesman was leading a group of his villagers hunting in the forests above the Monjar Khola. They would kill any animal they could find, to supplement a diet which lacks protein.

These chortens below Gatlang had a neglected look, and although there were other Buddhist symbols throughout the region, and a large gompa in Gatlang itself, this may be an area where Buddhism is in retreat before Hindu immigrants from the south.

This primitive bamboo fish trap in the Monjar Khola resembled similar traps seen elsewhere in Nepal. Although the rivers seem to contain few fish, the people also use simple rods and home-made nets.

The peak of Naya Kanga guards the approaches to the Kangja La, a pass from Langtang leading directly south toward Kathmandu, only 35 miles away. This was the route we had hoped to take, until two days and nights of heavy snowfall prevented us from taking our thinly-clad porters safely over the pass.

In the last few miles before joining the Trisuli River, the Langtang Khola enters an impassable gorge, walled by high cliffs and steep, thickly-wooded slopes. Few people may ever have penetrated this sanctuary, and it is in areas such as this that the "yeti" – if it exists – may live its secret life.

Falling from the
western end of
Langtang Himal, the
Pangsung Lekh drops
from over 19,500 feet to
the Langtang Khola at
only 6,500 feet, in little
over six miles. Beyond
the ridge, the valley of
the Trisuli River is a
route into Tibet which
may carry vehicles in
the not-too-distant
future.

TEMPLE
OF WOOD

The Indrapur and Krishna temples silhouetted against clouds

Flying into Nepal from Dacca in Bangladesh that first time, I did not guess that this was an experience to be repeated again and again. On that first visit, the Ganges plains were still deep in post-monsoon floods, and we flew north to where the pale brown waters lapped against the darker land, climbed to clear a mountain range, and nosed down through clouds into a green valley lying like a jewel in the hills. It was greener than anything I had ever seen, and at its heart lay a dust-brown city. This was Kathmandu, whose ancient name is the key to its origins, and whose people and rulers had raised three thousand temples to the gods they revered.

Today it is still a sacred city, and few would deny that Kathmandu possesses some very special qualities. It is idle to pretend that it does not also have beggars, smelly piles of garbage, persistent street vendors, carpet-baggers and get-rich-quick merchants. Hidden by a recent veneer of western-style commerce and service industries, it survives as the forbidden city which for millenia existed without the least influence from the West. This is the city of living goddesses, in the valley of 2,700 temples, where Buddhism and Hinduism are inextricably mixed, and the people are constant and devout in their beliefs.

To rise early and walk the streets of Kathmandu is to see a city at worship, in which thousands of people from all classes pay daily public homage to their chosen deity by performing a *puja*, or ceremony. Hindus will make small offerings of flowers, fruit, rice and coins, while murmuring prayers and incantations, while Buddhists may prostrate themselves a hundred times

Sacred cow
and Coca Cola
at Kamal Pokhri

before their chosen shrine. None of this is grafted on for the benefit of tourists or kept artificially alive by a "heritage" industry. It is an integral part of people's lives, set in a continuing culture, secure in its traditions and history.

Kathmandu is the crossroads for all who come to Nepal: Buddhists from around the world to the shrine of Swayambunath; Tibetan refugees to the other great Buddhist site at Bodnath; Hindus to their place of pilgrimage at Pasupatinath; Indian merchants; jet-setters on a world tour, and tourists of every kind, as well as trekkers, mountain lovers and mountain climbers. Kathmandu and the surrounding valley has something to offer them all.

Back in 1979, staying in Kathmandu before and after my trip to Khumbu, I was too taken up with the excitement of the expedition itself to pay much heed to the city. The Everest region had been busy with mountaineers: Doug Scott on Nuptse, a Polish expedition on Lhotse, a German/American expedition on Everest, Norman Deyrenfurth of Everest West Ridge fame making a film about Sherpa life, and others like myself with lesser objectives. I had encountered many of them on my Khumbu travels; meeting up with some of them again in Kathmandu I felt a little like a temporary member of a very exclusive club. My friend Mikame knew the members of a successful Japanese expedition to Dhaulagiri; the Burgess twins were in town, fresh from a climb in the Annapurnas.

Everywhere, it seemed – in the streets by day and in the restaurants at night – there were climbers, and all the talk was of mountains. A month later, returning from my second trip (to Annapurna) I found the city quieter. Winter had arrived and the mountaineers were gone. In the few days left before my flight home, waiting each morning for a cold, thick mist to clear, I began an exploration of the city which I now take up again each time I am there.

Simply to visit the famous shrines and temples of the Kathmandu Valley is a major project, and down every back street and alley more temples are hidden, and here also is the powerful throb of life that makes the city what it is. Here among the bazaars, the spice sellers, goldsmiths, silversmiths, woodcarvers, potters and the hundred other pliers of trades and crafts which flourish still, is the other side of that vital culture. For those who want it, there is another journey to be made here, through the world of Nepali art and architecture, and the genuine interest and patronage of visitors and tourists may well be important safeguards for the future of these arts.

In the decade of the eighties drastic physical changes were made

Saddhu at Kasta Mandap shrine

to Kathmandu, particularly the boom in hotel development and the loss of traditional architecture. As with much else in Nepal, the city needs a great deal of protection, perhaps more so than some other parts of the country. It is to be hoped that the same grouping of interests which is beginning to deal with problems in the countryside will not ignore Kathmandu.

There are other greater problems too. Writing this in the spring of 1990, Nepal and India have now been embroiled in a trade/border dispute for over a year, with no public signs of an early settlement, while recurring political demonstrations in Kathmandu itself have led to deaths and injuries. In April I was a sad and unwilling witness to repressive Government actions against people demonstrating in the name of democracy. It seems now, after great violence, that with the promise of elections they may have won a victory. Although the democratic movement has great popular support, reactionary forces are still at work; there is a long way to go, and the final outcome is hard to predict.

But the myth, cherished by many who thought they knew Nepal, of rediscovering here a lost age of innocence, is gone forever.

Stone Buddhas flank the stairs at the foot of Swayambunath Hill. Below the hill a growing community of Tibetan refugees has found a home, and each morning they can be seen at prayer in front of their protector.

Looking south from a rooftop below Swayambunath, Kathmandu sprawls across the valley. The city itself has a population of around 300,000; the Kathmandu Valley as a whole has 800,000, growing at more than 3 percent a year – too fast to be sustainable.

Walking a footpath on the northern outskirts of Kathmandu, a boy brings his family's produce to market. Originally given over to rice growing, the fertile soil of the valley can support three crops a year, and now also cultivates a great variety of fruit and vegetables for the many new hotels.

In a temple yard behind Durbar Square, a dispute was being debated where these men had gathered. This public hearing is something more commonly seen in the hill villages, where lack of access to the courts means that civil actions are often decided by debate.

In a doorway off Patan's Durbar Square, two men converse. The back streets of Kathmandu and its satellite towns, Patan and Bhadgaon, remain mostly a dark mystery to visitors.

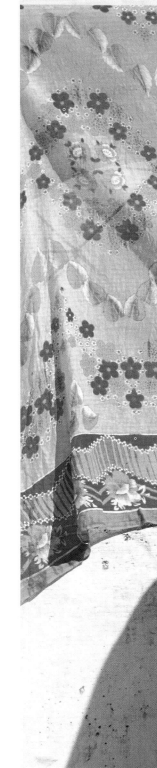

Spreading her sari to dry on a wall by the city's national theatre, right in the middle of Kathmandu, this Hindu woman was oblivious to the dust and the traffic speeding by only yards away.

Surrounded by his goods, the spice seller sits in the Asan bazaar just off Indrachowk, in the heart of old Kathmandu. The streets and squares hum with the life of the bazaar by day; after dark they are almost deserted.

The god Vishnu, in the form of Narayan, lies on a bed made from the coils of the serpent, Ananta. This masterpiece of Licchavi art from around the sixth century lies in the village of Budanilkanth, at the foot of the Shivapuri Hills, some five miles north of Kathmandu.

The huge and complex shrine at Pasupatinath straddles the sacred Bagmati River, three miles east of Kathmandu. Dedicated to Shiva in his benign form as god of animals, the temples and dharmasalas (shelters for pilgrims) lie near the site of Deopatan, capital of the ancient Licchavi civilization.

This beggar waited a long time for a hand-out at the end of Kathmandu's New Road, constructed after the great earthquake of 1934.

Begging is not institutionalized in Nepal, as it has become in India, although both Hindus and Buddhists gain merit by the giving of alms.

The sky is heavy with late monsoon clouds behind the shrine of Swayambunath, seen from Kaldhara on the outskirts of Kathmandu. Known to have existed for more than 2,500 years, the shrine was destroyed in the fourteenth century by Moslem armies from Bengal. It was later restored and today is of great importance to Buddhists the world over.

On the hilltop at Swayambu, the stupa has pride of place among other shrines, Buddhist and Hindu. The four faces of the stupa look north, south, east and west to symbolize the all-seeing Buddha.

A stone staircase of 300 steps leads to the shrine of Swayambu, just outside Kathmandu to the west. As the early sun penetrates the morning mists, a beggar waits for the devotees who will soon appear for their daily ascent to the hilltop shrine.

146

Just over a mile from Pasupatinath, the great stupa at Bodnath has become the heart of Tibetan life and culture in Nepal, which houses many refugees from Chinese repression in Tibet. Around the stupa cluster monasteries and theological schools, private shrines and chapels as well as homes, shops and souvenir stalls.

Wood carving adorns buildings all around the Kathmandu Valley, from elaborate temple decorations like these in Patan, to the elegant carved doors and windows of traditional homes. Much of the best carving dates from the flowering of the Malla civilization in the fifteenth and sixteenth centuries, when many Nepalese arts achieved levels never surpassed since.

149

Kimdol, on the western outskirts of Kathmandu, emerges through the early mists which fill the valley throughout the autumn and winter. Even on cold mornings, however, these mists are soon dispersed as the sun gets higher in the sky.

EAST OF THE MOON

Chamlang (left) and Makalu 40 miles away

It is autumn 1988 and I have come to Nepal with an old friend and veteran of several Arctic expeditions, Iain Roy; it is his first visit to the Himalayas, and we are on a four-week trek to Makalu, to the east of Everest.

Today the sun shines and a hot wind blows all the way from the Bay of Bengal, staying with us throughout the day until our rendezvous with the Arun River. It is with us during the next few days too, keeping them hot, and in the afternoons building great piles of cumulous over the hills.

Along this trail bloom hibiscus, poinsettia, frangipani; outside every house a drift of orange marigolds, sacred to both Hindu and Buddhist. Between villages we walk the flood course of the river on gravel bars and beaches of grey, glacial sand; there are grassy meadows, reed beds, rushes, stands of sugar cane. In the fields the main crop is rice, but there is also millet, wheat and barley, and by the houses, leaf and root vegetables.

The trails are busy – this week is the festival of Dasaain, and women and children have made the traditional journey to their mother's home; groups of men have been as far as Dharan or even Kathmandu. All are now returning to their villages. The people of the low valleys here are Newars, Rais, Limbus, Magars; higher, there are Brahmin and Chetris; the hill tribes are Thamangs, Sherpas and Bhotias. We see them all here on this path; most with a friendly greeting and the clear, direct look of country people everywhere.

At night we camp on sandy flats beside the river. The Arun glides past with deceptive, silky power. It is too cold to swim in, and the current too strong; we look for warmer streams to wash the day's dust from our clothes, and to ease tired bodies. Twilight is short; an evening meal prepared and eaten, our porters murmur around the fire; in the warm darkness of the tent, sleep comes quickly.

Mid-morning the next day, and the heat builds up. Below a solitary banyan tree on a hillock sit two small girls, selling green tangerines, tart and delicious, four for one rupee. Later, in the greater heat of mid-afternoon, we come across a funeral party carrying a wrapped corpse to the burial place. Far from being mournful, they are cheerful – it turns out they are tipsy. The large vessels they carry contain not funeral sacraments but chang – rice beer – and when we are pressed to try some it is cool and refreshing; we need no encouragement to take more.

Village children during the Dasaain festival

From Num, a village of ten houses and two stores, we must descend 3,000 feet to cross the Arun. Over the bridge we swing northwest and climb away from the river, heading into hilly country and the first real intimations of the mountains to come. Rocky outcrops and fast-flowing streams punctuate the slopes above us, and when we sit for half an hour to rest the skies fill with a parade of the great raptors – golden eagle, griffon, red and black kite, harrier and falcon. The day's trail crosses open slopes of winter barley and, elsewhere, abandoned terraces and hamlets.

In the afternoon, the first cloud forest: oak, giant

Corn store,
Arun Valley

rhododendron, pine and cedar. The undergrowth is dense; ferns fill any space between the trees, moss hangs from the branches and orchids grow profusely. To be alone for a while in these surroundings, I walk quickly away from the others. In a green cathedral, cool and dark, sounds are muted. A ray of sunshine penetrates, as if through stained glass; the air is still.

The following day we climb just four hours to a dank clearing in the rhododendron forest, since the next water is too far off for our porters. Deep in the trees, we lose the sun early and it is soon cold. Far down the darkening valley a lamp gleams, a dog barks. At night the ground is hard and sleep difficult. In the morning a heavy dew has soaked the tents and Iain and I stride off ahead of the porters, for it is colder now and we need movement to keep warm. On the open ridge above the trees, as we cross a couple of false summits, a cold wind sighs across the rocks. But the next summit is the final one; 300 feet below, a black pond nestles in a hollow on the ridge.

By bedtime flakes of snow swirl out of the darkness and into the circle of light around our fire. The porters huddle closer to the flames, muttering and hugging themselves; we share their unease. But in the morning the sun is shining brightly from a blue sky and far on the eastern horizon Kangchenjunga and Jannu rise above the sea of cloud which laps against our ridge. In little over an hour we stand on the crest of Shipton's Col. The altitude is 14,000 feet and to the north, beyond another col, lie the Barun Valley and the peaks of Tibet. Over the last ridge the trail plunges 3,000 feet to the Barun Khola, in a steep and agonizing descent.

The valley is wild and wonderful, and the river a rush of green water past great stands of conifers. Above us are soaring cliffs; to the north and west, snow peaks. An hour or so upstream, camp is made in a small meadow, Tematan Kharka, flanked by pines and backed by tall cliffs. Next day at Nehe Kharka – Sacred Meadow – two roofless huts and a flutter of prayer flags are the marks of sometime human presence in this valley; in summer cattle will be driven up here for the lush grazing. A solitary yak has strayed and watches us file past.

The glaciers of Peak Seven loom above ice-worn cliffs; a blunt wedge seamed with ice rises into cloud. We cross the river on a narrow two-log bridge – bank to boulder, boulder to far bank – and plunge into pine woods. Under the trees, rhododendrons hide seams of old snow; clearwater streams rush down across the path; pine needles shiver at our passing. At dusk we emerge above the treeline to camp at 14,000 feet, among patches of juniper, seeking the shelter of a large boulder for our fire and tents as more snow sweeps down from Tibet.

Too high for permanent human settlement, and too remote for animals often to be hunted, the Barun Valley is a sanctuary for species harried almost to extinction elsewhere. Close by the tents a pair of wolves has left clear traces in the snow. At daybreak we follow the tracks to where they cross a stream – thin ice broken below the banks – and, above, another set of marks comes down the hillside. The hairs rise on my neck, for these are the tracks of a cat; but they are too small for snow leopard and must be lynx. Higher, a fox has crossed the trail; nearby, a hare has swung away with lengthening strides; in long grass, barely covered by the snow, a tiny, hopping creature leaves a curiously touching imprint.

Ahead the trail descends to a flat, boulder-strewn area, hemmed between glacier and valley wall, before a sudden narrowing leaves space only for the river between piled moraines and low cliffs. We turn the corner of the crags on icy stones in silty water. The valley turns abruptly north and widens, and a broad alluvial plain runs to the base of low, brown hills whose summits brush the cloud base. On the fourteenth day of walking we are at Sherson. Makalu is hidden in those clouds – a palpable presence – and a temporary thinning of the mist gives hints of towering rock and ice.

Dropping my pack, I walk another mile, cross the Barun Khola on icy boulders, and climb the lateral moraine above the South Barun Glacier. At the rim the glacier lies a hundred feet

Iain, Nima and porters, Barun Valley

below; a blue and jagged ice fall tumbles between Peak Four and Chamlang and the glacial lake we saw is far behind. Cloud swirls around the summits; mist forms and melts; an ice slope glistens; peaks vanish – all is deep silence. Breaking the spell I turn and walk down to meet the others; in the distance, Nima waves.

Late in the afternoon the veil of northern cloud is very slowly lifted. A sweep of curved ridge leads to a shining summit whose grace and symmetry leave no room for doubt that this is Makalu, fifth highest mountain in the world. We watch until the last rays of the setting sun burn on the highest rocks, then fade. At dusk the mountain is palest rose against deepening blue; the landscape lies in darkness.

In the night, waking to the distant howl of a wolf, I quietly don boots and coat and slip out of the tent. A haloed moon lifts over Peak Six and the plain of Sherson lies silent and empty. The frost is fierce. Above all, Makalu raises coldly gleaming snows into the glimmering sky.

The north face of
Chamlang rises almost
directly from the plain
of Sherson. On the walk
in, we had met some
members of a small
German expedition
who had failed to get
higher than 20,000 feet
on the peak, but still
described the
experience as the
greatest of their lives.

Although just a day's walk from the airstrip at Tumlingtar, the regional centre of Khandbari is five days from the nearest road. Walking up the Arun River, this is the last village to have electricity, supplied from a hydroelectric power scheme in the lower valley.

This Rai woman, cutting sweet grass for her buffalo, had wandered over to our tents out of curiosity. Nepalese women have a natural grace and wonderful sense of style, seen at its best in their festival attire, but apparent in their everyday clothes too.

Only the buffalo, tethered outside their owner's home at Tumlingtar, were awake as we stopped to rest in the shade after a steep climb. On uphill stretches, even at seven in the morning, the sun seemed punishingly hot.

On the outskirts of Num, the last village on the south bank of the Arun River, a new house was nearly finished. We had stopped here for a day to rest, wash and find new porters, since our ever-smiling Rai porters from Hille felt they had come far enough and were anxious to return home.

The tailor at Sultibari represents one of the two mechanized trades found in the smaller villages in Nepal. Both the tailor and the typist may serve an entire region. The other tradesman occasionally seen is the blacksmith – still viewed by many villagers with awe.

We sought shelter from the fierce midday heat in this grain store at the edge of rice paddies in the Arun Valley. Tightly thatched against the monsoon rains, the store was open-walled for ventilation, and the farmer's tools tidily stored in the roof timbers.

Air temperatures in the upper Barun Valley, at 15,000 feet, rarely rose much above freezing during our stay in November. Small side streams would be reduced to a trickle overnight, as their sources higher up froze nearly solid, reaching full flow again only in mid-afternoon.

This Bhotia woman, from a town on the Tibetan border, was dressed in her finest clothes for the second-last day of Divali, Festival of Lights. As we passed through the village of Seduwa, on our return, a market was being held and gambling (legal only on this one day of the year) was in full swing.

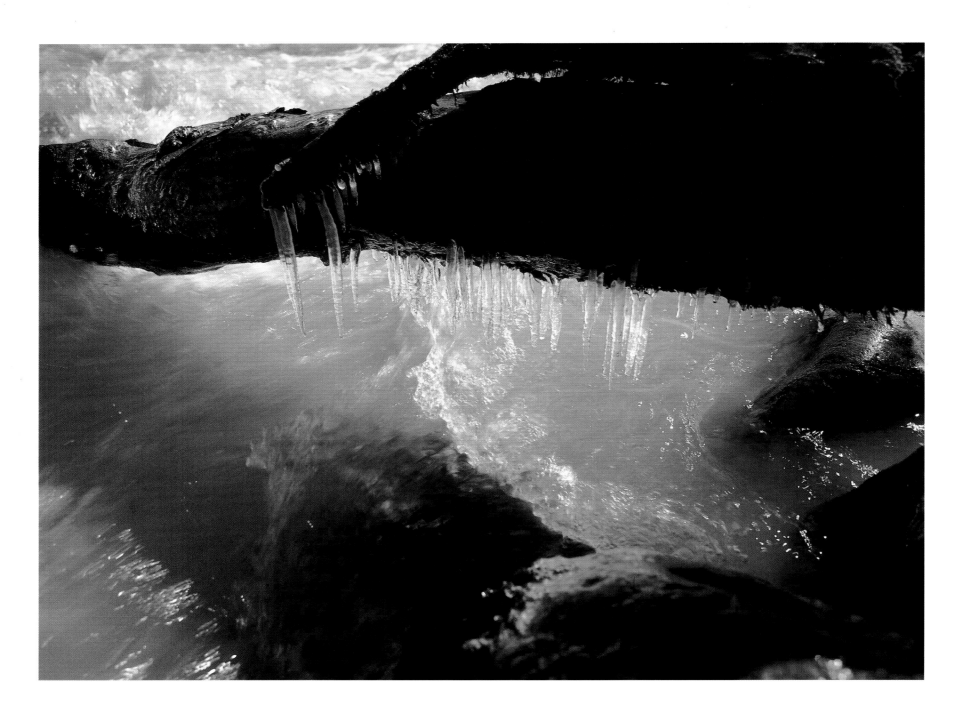

The giant ferns stirred in the faintest breeze on the fringes of the forests below Tashigaon, the last village on our walk to Makalu. Bird calls were muted by the dense foliage and the only other sound was the rustle of falling leaves.

Widely available throughout the warm regions of Nepal, bananas are a welcome addition to the trekker's diet. After periods up in the mountains, it is a relief to find fresh fruit and vegetables on the walk back.

About halfway on the descent from Shipton's Col into the Barun Valley we reached the treeline once again. The highest ridges had been bare of all except rough grass and low-growing alpine succulents. A little lower the vegetation was dense rhododendron bushes, and as we reached the pines the landscape was reminiscent of Canada.

Mist swirled around the peaks on our last morning at Sherson, dissipating and reforming in seconds above the ice fall north of Chamlang. On a day without a trace of wind, the only sound was an occasional rattle of stones from the glacier below.

Iain comes up the side of the South Barun Glacier on our last morning. Back down at Sherson, Nima was getting ready to break camp and set off down the Barun Valley to join most of our porters at a warmer camp site.

In the lower reaches of the valley, the Barun Khola is a wide, fast-flowing stream whose noise made conversation difficult. The steep southern slopes were extremely loose, and the trail often ran below great boulders poised above shifting scree and sand, making walking there a scary experience.

Afternoon mists begin to gather below our camp at Sherson, an alluvial plain at the top end of the Barun Valley. As soon as the sun went down it was numbingly cold, an experience intensified by the freezing mist.

173

We had come a long way to see Makalu, and almost never did. Problems with permits in Kathmandu, illness on the trail and porter troubles had all delayed us and made us abandon many of our earlier ambitions. Just to reach Sherson and see Makalu became our only goal. Even this was almost denied us by the weather, but we were finally rewarded.

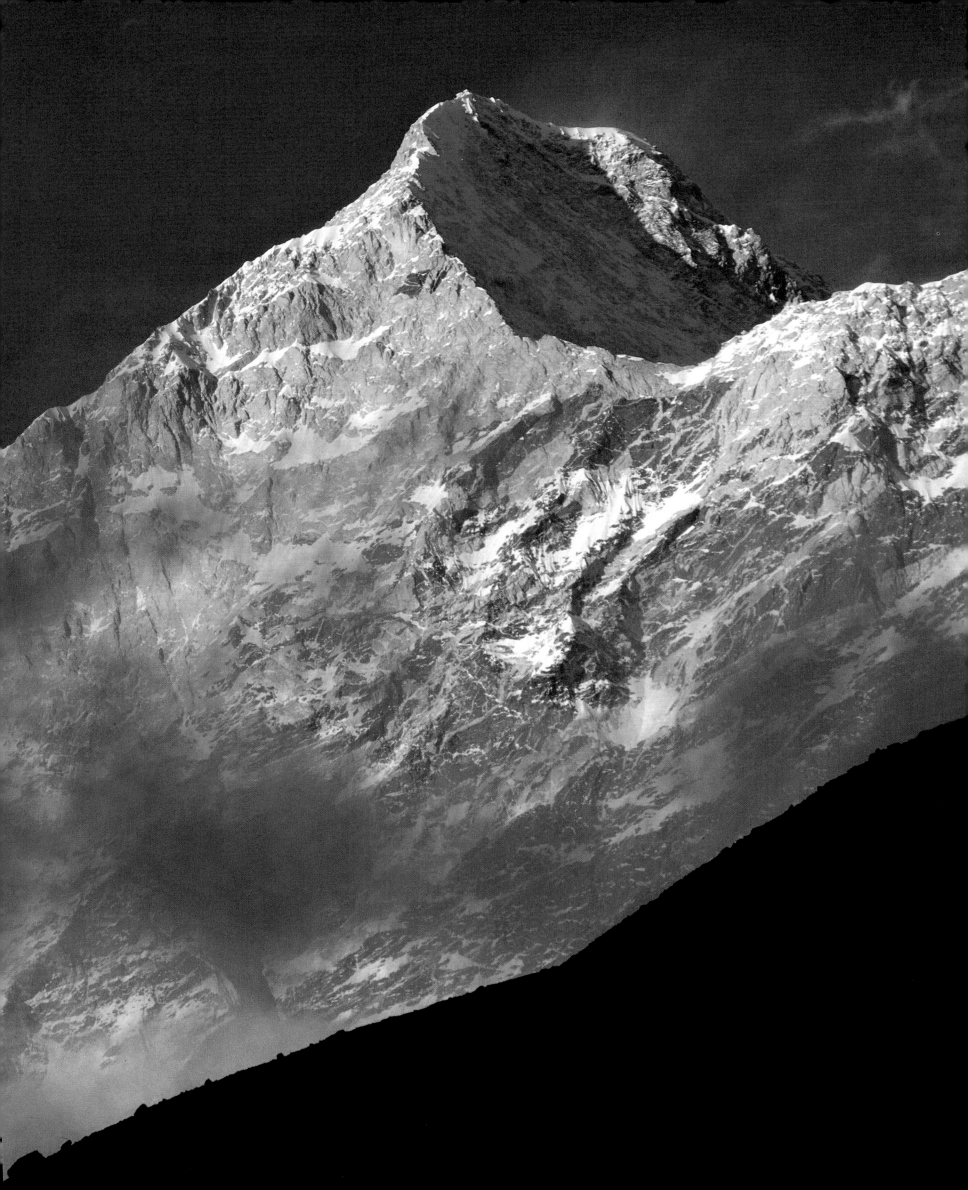

This is the traveller's dream.

For a lucky few, it has also been reality in recent years. But the people of these hills are vulnerable, and the ecosystems which sustain them are precious and fragile; both can be all too easily damaged. Such damage is rarely reversible. If the dream is to continue and the people of Nepal, who give so much and ask so little in return, are to lead the lives they deserve – in the hills they love – much needs to be done. Not least, every visitor who is privileged enough to come here must understand how great the privilege is, and how easily it may be removed. We must all strive to preserve and protect the treasures we have come to admire.

Nima Wangchu Sherpa

SPECIAL THANKS

I owe a lot to Kiyotomo Mikame for his initial help and encouragement. One thing he did had special significance – he introduced me to Nima Wangchu Sherpa from Karikhola in the Solu district south of Khumbu. We struck up an immediate friendship, which has lasted until now. Although I could have made these journeys without him, I might have looked a long time to find his equal: resourceful, knowledgeable, with a quiet humour and a gentle way with porters and the country people of Nepal. I look forward to many other treks and climbs with Nima.

Within Marshall Editions, my thanks must go to Zilda Tandy, whose enthusiasm for the project got it going, and to Bruce Marshall and his directors for their continuing belief in it.

My family, Mayumi and Sean, rarely grumbled at my absences, and were always pleased to have me home again – which is all that the selfish traveller can ask.